Welcome to our reverse colorin creativity knows no bounds!

This book is designed to provide a unique and engaging coloring experience that encourages you to think outside the lines and unleash your inner artist.

Reverse coloring is a new and exciting technique that allows you to explore the art of coloring in a whole new way. Instead of coloring within the lines of a pre-drawn design, reverse coloring involvescoloring around the outlines of a beautiful, abstract shape, revealing a stunning and unique work of art. Within these pages, you'll find a collection of intricate designs inspired by animals, landscapes, nature, and abstract watercolors. Each design has been carefully crafted to provide you with a challenging and rewarding coloring experience that will ignite your creativity and inspire your imagination.

Happy coloring!

Tips and Tricks

Use a fine-tipped pen: When creating your outline, use a pen with a fine tip to ensure that your lines are crisp and clean.
You can also experiment with different types of pens to create different line widths and textures.

Basic shapes: If you're feeling stuck or overwhelmed, start by drawing basic shapes like circles, squares, and triangles.
These shapes can serve as the building blocks for more complex drawings.

Use different coloring tools: Don't be afraid to experiment with different coloring tools, such as markers, colored pencils, or watercolors. Each tool has its own unique properties and can create different effects on the page.

Play with shading: Create depth and dimension by using shading techniques. Start by coloring the areas closest to the center of the design with darker shades and gradually work your way out with lighter shades. You can also use crosshatching, stippling, or other shading techniques to add texture and interest.

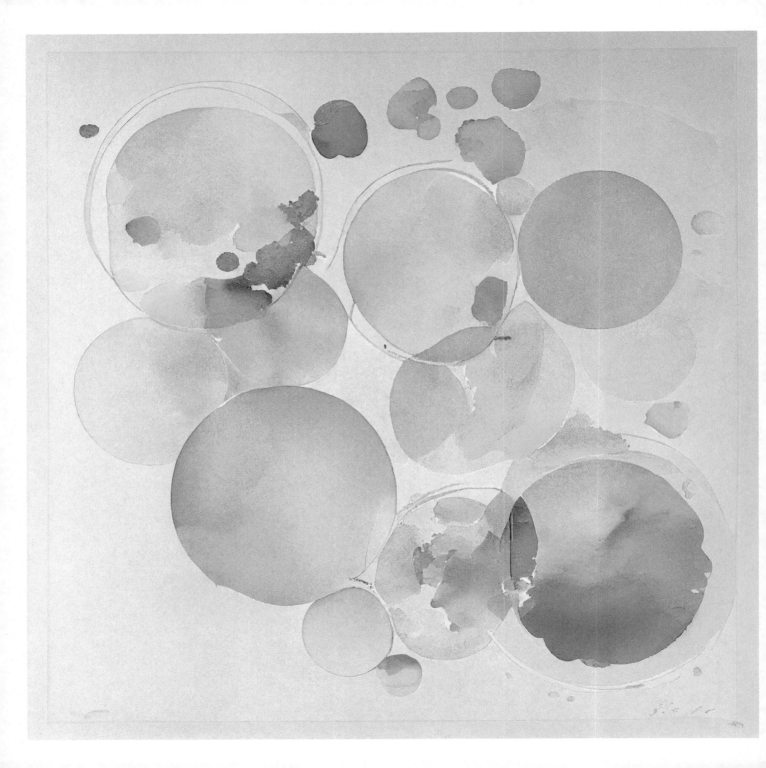

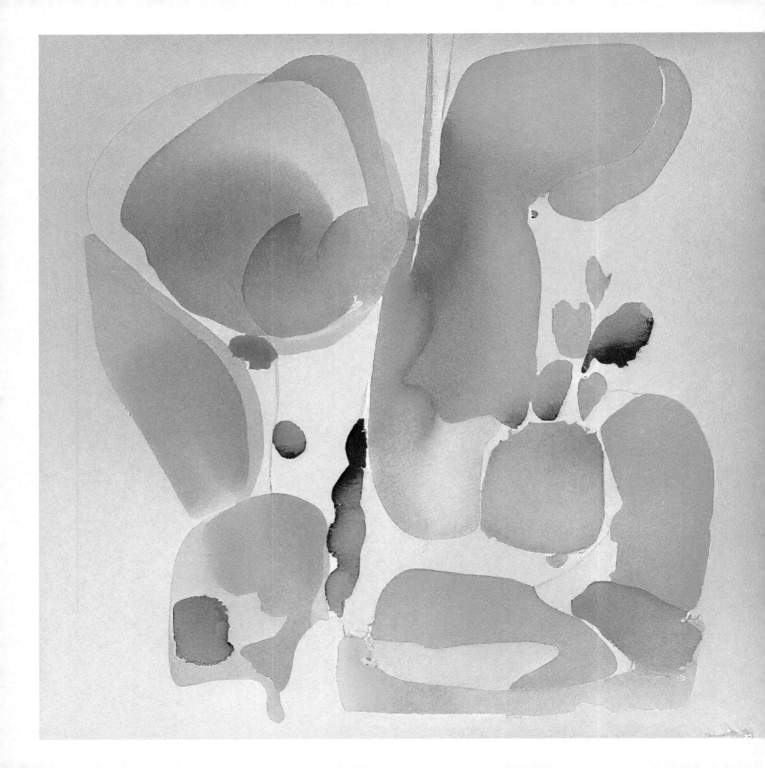

Thank you for choosing our reverse coloring book and taking a journey through our watercolor designs.

We hope our book has sparked your creativity and brought you some moments of relaxation and joy.

If you enjoyed our book, please consider leaving a review, your feedback can help us improve and inspire others to try reverse coloring.

Stay tuned for our upcoming volume, which will showcase even more intricate and fascinating artwork. We can't wait to see what you'll create next.

Happy coloring!
Brush & Color Press

Printed in Great Britain
by Amazon

46176622R00044